My Unique ADHD World

Joanne Steer & Claire Berry

Illustrated by Abigail Tompkins

Jessica Kingsley Publishers

London and Philadelphia

Foreword

Hopefully a book like this will help others who might have friends or family who have ADHD. Some people just don't get it or understand.

As a child with ADHD sometimes school can be challenging so it is helpful for other people around me to understand what I like and dislike. Knowing what I like and dislike means others can help me focus my attention on these interests. Those with ADHD have lots of strengths; I have lots of energy and my friends find me funny.

I have already forgotten what I'm supposed to write.

I find it difficult to concentrate for long periods of time and get easily distracted, so I will conclude here and go back to cuddling my cat and playing my video games.

Oliver Steer, aged 11

Acknowledgments

To my amazing family for all their love and support, from Jo.

To all the young people and families I have worked with over the years who have enhanced my knowledge of ADHD. To my family for always encouraging and supporting me, from Claire.

Introduction

Every person with ADHD is unique. In this book lots of children will tell you about their ADHD.

ADHD stands for Attention Deficit Hyperactivity Disorder. You don't need to remember the full name as most people call it ADHD. Having ADHD means that your brain works a bit differently. We aren't sure exactly why this is; however, we know that ADHD runs in families so if you have ADHD it's likely someone else in your family may have it as well, such as your parent, grandparent, or aunt or uncle. There is also some science that says people with ADHD have brains that don't produce enough of a chemical called Dopamine. This can make the brain work much faster so you notice lots of things that are going on around you. This can also mean you get distracted more easily and find it hard to concentrate.

It is important that you understand more about ADHD. In this book we have included some interesting facts about ADHD for you to read and share with people.

Everyone has things they are good at and things they find more difficult. ADHD can give you some special strengths; however, it can also make some things more difficult. It is helpful for you to understand **your unique ADHD**, so you can recognize your own strengths and difficulties. Have a look through the book and think about whether you notice the same things happening to you?

Let's explore what ADHD means for you.

WHAT DO I ALREADY KNOW ABOUT ADHD?

Write or draw in the box what you already know about ADHD.

I love to daydream and spend time creating stories in my mind. Sometimes this means I get into trouble if I should have been listening to a grownup!

FACT: Lots of children have ADHD! There will be children in your school who have ADHD but you may not know it.

I am forgetful and I often forget to bring home my water bottle or jumper from school. I can even forget what I have just been asked or was about to say in a conversation.

I always seem to lose things, even my most special toys! This is really annoying and people have to help me find my things.

I am great at thinking quickly and in an emergency I am the best at making a quick plan.

FACT: Both boys and girls can have ADHD.

I get distracted very easily, so when I am supposed to be getting dressed for school, I end up jumping on my bed!

This means I am sometimes late for school or get into trouble.

I have trouble finishing things I have started. I start watching films, drawing pictures or my homework and end up doing something else and never finishing them.

I can spend a really long time doing an activity I love, like reading a book or playing a video game. Sometimes I don't realize how long I have spent doing these things. It does mean that I have become really good at these things and know lots about them.

FACT: Adults have ADHD too.

I don't like doing things where I have to sit and concentrate for a long time. I try to put off starting my schoolwork and take a while to settle down and get on with it. I also rush my work just to get it finished quickly.

Rushing my work means I get the answers wrong or make spelling mistakes, even though I know how to spell the words!

I find it really hard to concentrate on things.

When I am watching a TV programme or talking to someone I lose my focus and end up missing part of the conversation or TV show. This does make it hard to listen and follow what people are saying to me.

I find it hard to follow instructions. If my teacher tells me to get my book out, read a page in the book and then write down what I have read about, I often find that I can get my book out, but will forget what I need to do next.

FACT: Did you know the amazing Olympic American gymnast Simone Biles has ADHD?

I have lots of energy, more than most people I know!

I love being active and doing things like riding my scooter, bouncing on trampolines or just running!

I have so much energy and this makes it hard to sit still.
When I go somewhere, such as the cinema, I move around
lots in my seat and always want to get out of my chair.

I like to talk lots and am called a chatterbox. I am great at telling lots of interesting stories which other people enjoy listening to.

FACT: More people are being diagnosed with ADHD. This is because we understand ADHD much better now.

I have a great sense of humour and people say I am really funny.

I find it hard to do things quietly so when my teacher asks me to work in silence I start humming or singing.

I am full of energy and have creative ideas!
This can make me fun to be around.

FACT: ADHD girls are more likely to daydream, and ADHD boys are more likely to have lots of energy – but sometimes it's the other way around. Everyone is unique!

I am really competitive and always want to win games, so it is really hard to wait for my turn.

I am brilliant at coming up with different ideas – I invent new games and really exciting stories or draw characters that no one has ever thought of before.

I do things without thinking, which often end up in me hurting myself, such as walking out into the road without looking or climbing up a very high tree.

I feel I have to say something out loud as soon as I have thought of it. I often call out the answer to a question in class without waiting to be asked by the teacher or I find it hard to wait my turn when someone else is talking.

I don't need very much sleep; I fall asleep quite late and wake up early.

I notice that some things such as noises, bright lights, smells and the feel and taste of things make me feel uncomfortable or stressed.

FACT: People used to think that ADHD meant you couldn't focus on anything. We now know that it can also mean people can focus for a really long time on things they are interested in. This is called hyperfocus.

I get angry, upset or excited very quickly and it can take a while for me to feel calm again.